World Geography Quick Starts

Editor: Mary Dieterich
Proofreaders: Margaret Brown and April Albert

COPYRIGHT © 2019 Mark Twain Media, Inc.

ISBN 978-1-62223-777-7

Printing No. CD-405043

Mark Twain Media, Inc., Publishers
Distributed by Carson-Dellosa Publishing LLC

Visit www.carsondellosa.com

Table of Contents

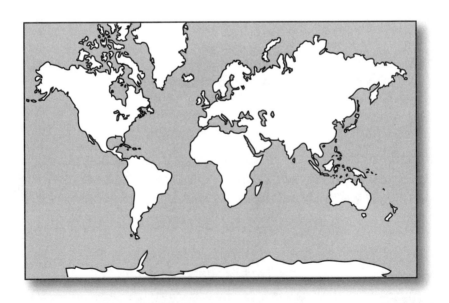

Introduction to the Teacher

World Geography Quick Starts offers teachers and parents short quick start activities to help students practice and apply the map skills and geography knowledge they have learned in their social studies classes. Used at the beginning of class, these mini-tasks help students focus on understanding geography concepts when applied to the study of the continents of the world.

The pages are grouped into units covering basic geography terms and map skills, as well as units focusing on each of the continents. Each continent unit features quick starts highlighting the geography concepts of location, place, human-environment interaction, movement, and region.

The quick start activities allow students to use a variety of map skills, such as finding directions, utilizing latitude and longitude coordinates, using map legends and scales, and identifying physical features. Other activities focus on recalling information about the continents, such as countries and capitals, languages and customs of the people, climate regions, and natural resources found around the world.

Two to four quick starts are included on each page. Reproduce the pages and cut along the lines, then use each section as a ten-minute quick start to the day's lesson, or distribute copies of uncut pages so students can keep their completed exercises in a three-ring binder for reference. Pages can also be kept in a learning center for students to work on when they have extra time. Either enlarged individual sections or uncut pages make excellent transparencies to share with the class.

Provide students with a world atlas or access to an online atlas. Some activities may require another sheet of paper for student responses.

World Geography Quick Starts supports the Geography for Life: National Geography Standards. Also, the book has been correlated to current state and national standards.

Geography Terms & Map Skills

Geography Terms & Map Skills 1

A **map** is a flat two-dimensional drawing of an area such as a city, a country, an ocean, or a continent. It shows the physical features as they would appear if you looked at them from above.

Identify the directions indicated by each side of the map below: **north**, **south**, **east**, **west**.

_____

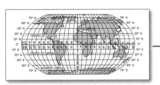

_____   _____

_____

Geography Terms & Map Skills 2

A **globe** is a three-dimensional representation of the earth, shaped like a ball or sphere. There is a grid system on a globe that is used to identify any location on the earth.

1. Lines of _____ run vertically from the North Pole to the South Pole.

2. Lines of _____ run horizontally around the globe from the equator up to the North Pole and down to the South Pole.

Geography Terms & Map Skills 3

Draw a line from each term to the correct drawing of that item.

1. map scale

A.

2. compass rose

B.

3. map key or legend

C.

Geography Terms & Map Skills 4

Match the geographical terms with the correct locations for each item.

____ 1. North Pole
____ 2. South Pole
____ 3. Equator
____ 4. Prime Meridian
____ 5. International Date Line
____ 6. Northern Hemisphere
____ 7. Eastern Hemisphere

A. 0° latitude   **B.** 180° longitude
C. 0° longitude   **D.** 90° S lat.
E. 90° N lat.   **F.** 0–180° E long.
G. 0–90° N lat.

Geography Terms & Map Skills

Geography Terms & Map Skills 5

There are many different types of maps. Fill in the blanks to identify the types of maps described below.

1. A _____ map shows the man-made borders of countries, states, and so on.
2. A _____ use map shows how an area is used, such as for agriculture or mining.
3. A _____ map shows the features of an area, such as rivers, mountains, and plains.
4. A _____ map shows the highways present in an area.

Geography Terms & Map Skills 6

1. The scale on a map indicates that 1 inch equals 100 miles. Five inches on the map equals _____ miles.
2. The scale on a map indicates that 1 inch equals 25 kilometers. Three inches on the map equals _____ kilometers.
3. The scale on a map indicates that 1 inch equals 7 miles. 4.5 inches on the map equals _____ miles.

Geography Terms & Map Skills 7

Label the hemispheres below. Write the names on or near the hemispheres.

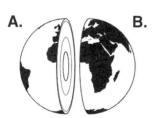
A.   B.

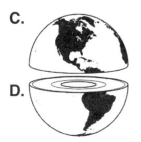
C.

D.

Geography Terms & Map Skills 8

Unscramble these words associated with maps.

1. LECSA _____
2. TEDALUIT _____
3. APCSOMS _____
4. GDELEN _____
5. OLCITIPLA _____
6. SPHLIACY _____
7. NIUEDLGOT _____
8. REDSEGE _____
9. OESRDRB _____
10. NOCASE _____

Geography Terms & Map Skills

Geography Terms & Map Skills 9

Label the lines of latitude from the equator to the poles. Each line is an increment of 15 degrees.

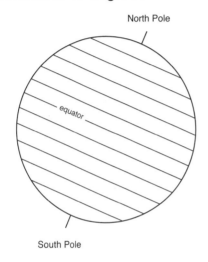

Geography Terms & Map Skills 10

Label the lines of longitude from the Prime Meridian to the International Date Line in the Eastern Hemisphere. Each line is an increment of 15 degrees.

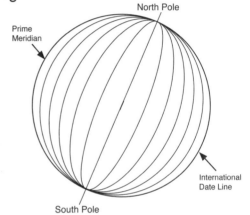

Geography Terms & Map Skills 11

The **absolute location** is the exact latitude and longitude coordinates of a place. The location is found by identifying the latitude of the place first and then the longitude. These two numbers form a coordinate pair that identify the exact location on a map or globe grid.

What city is found at each absolute location? Use a print or online atlas.

1. 42° N, 88° W _____
2. 34° S, 18° E _____
3. 60° N, 25° E _____
4. 33° S, 71° W _____

Geography Terms & Map Skills 12

Use a map of the United States. Write the correct direction to travel between the states listed. Use N (north); NE (northeast); E (east); SE (southeast); S (south); SW (southwest); W (west); or NW (northwest).

1. Wyoming to Montana _____
2. Idaho to California _____
3. Oklahoma to Tennessee _____
4. Utah to Arizona _____
5. Kansas to Iowa _____
6. Georgia to Mississippi _____
7. Alabama to Virginia _____
8. Texas to Oregon _____

Africa

Africa 1

The **relative location** of a place is found by describing it in relation to other places. It is like giving directions using landmarks.

Using a map of Africa, identify the country described below.

1. Large island to the east of Mozambique _____

2. Country in the northwest corner of Africa, separated from Spain by the Strait of Gibraltar _____

3. Country at the sourthern tip of Africa _____

Africa 2

Using a map of Africa, describe the relative locations of these physical features on your own paper. (What countries are they in or near? What surrounds them?)

1. Lake Victoria
2. Drakensberg Mountains
3. Kalahari Desert
4. Gulf of Guinea
5. Nile River

Africa 3

Using a map of Africa, give the absolute location (latitude and longitude) for the following places in Africa.

1. Algiers, Algeria _____
2. Khartoum, Sudan _____
3. Casablanca, Morocco _____
4. Lusaka, Zambia _____
5. Freetown, Sierra Leone _____
6. Cape of Good Hope _____
7. Lake Victoria _____
8. Mt. Kilimanjaro _____

Africa 4

Using a map of Africa or other resources, identify in which country or countries each of the following landmarks resides.

1. Okavango Delta _____
2. Serengeti National Park _____
3. Victoria Falls _____ _____
4. Pyramids of Giza _____
5. Lalibela _____
6. Lake Malawi _____ _____

Africa

Africa 5

Africa is a place of many different climates, but it is best known for the extreme climates of deserts and rain forests. Use a map of Africa or other resources. Indicate whether each place below is a desert (D) or a rain forest (R).

1. Danakil ____
2. Upper Guinea ____
3. Nyungwe ____
4. Namib ____
5. Congo Basin ____
6. Nigeria-Cameroon ____
7. Sahara ____
8. Kalahari ____

Africa 6

The Sahara Desert in northern Africa is the largest desert in the world. Using a print or online physical map of Africa, list at least five countries included in the area of the Sahara Desert.

_____

_____

_____

_____

_____

Africa 7

Many animals live in Africa's savannas. Unscramble the animals listed below.

1. EBZAR _____
2. IOLN _____
3. ECTHEHA _____
4. PTEELHNA _____
5. FGRIAFE _____
6. GOTWRAH _____
7. ZGLEALE _____
10. CRTSOIH _____

Africa 8

Many deep lakes are located along the Great Rift Valley in Eastern Africa where the continent is slowly being split apart. Unscramble the following lakes.

1. AKNTNYGAAI

_____

2. YAAAB _____
3. HOMCA _____
4. UTNAKRA _____
5. NTROAN _____
6. ARBLET _____
7. LWMAAI _____
8. DADEWR _____

Africa

Africa 9

Match these natural resources found in Africa to their uses. Use print or online resources to help you, if needed.

____	**1.** chromite	**A.** rare hardwood
____	**2.** bauxite	**B.** minerals used for fertilizer
____	**3.** mahogany	**C.** fossil fuel
____	**4.** phosphates	**D.** used for the hardening of steel
____	**5.** coal	**E.** ore from which aluminum is extracted

Africa 10

Anthropologists divide traditional African society into major types based on their primary activity. Based on the names of these societies, describe what they do and in what type of environment they likely live.

1. hunters _____

_____

2. fishers _____

_____

3. planters _____

_____

Africa 11

The actions of humans often have effects on the environment. Next to each sentence, write *C* if it is a cause of desertification in Africa or *R* if it is a result of desertification.

____	**1.** clearing land for cultivation	____	**2.** animal poaching
____	**3.** creeping sand buries towns	____	**4.** war
____	**5.** climate changes/drought	____	**6.** stripping trees for fuel
____	**7.** erosion of topsoil by wind	____	**8.** overgrazing of land
____	**9.** nomads must settle in towns	____	**10.** famine

Africa

Africa 12

Match the type of African art to its description.

____ **1.** Kente cloth
____ **2.** call and response
____ **3.** oral tradition
____ **4.** masks
____ **5.** northern art

A. told by one generation to the next
B. used in ceremonies and rituals
C. special design once reserved for royalty
D. influenced by Islam
E. a leader sings a phrase and the chorus repeats the phrase

Africa 13

The rivers of Africa provide vital routes for the movement of people and goods. Using a print or online map of Africa, match each river to its general location.

____ **1.** Nile   **A.** South Africa
____ **2.** Congo   **B.** Northeastern Africa
____ **3.** Zambezi
____ **4.** Orange   **C.** West-central Africa
____ **5.** Niger
               D. Central Africa
               E. Southeastern Africa

Africa 14

Using online or print resources, find the top imports and exports for each African nation.

	Import	Export
1. Niger	____	____
2. Kenya	____	____
3. Egypt	____	____
4. Botswana	____	____
5. Morocco	____	____
6. Togo	____	____
7. South Africa	____	____
8. Libya	____	____

Africa 15

People, ideas, languages, governments, and products often moved across Africa as European nations colonized the continent. Identify which European nation had control of each African country in the past.

1. Algeria _____
2. Zambia _____
3. Ethiopia _____
4. Western Sahara _____
5. Democratic Republic of the Congo _____
6. Tanzania _____
7. Angola _____

Africa

Africa 16

The Suez Canal, completed in 1869, had an important impact on the movement of people, products, and ideas through the region. Goods and people could move much quicker from west to east or east to west. The control of the canal also led to tensions and fighting because it was in such a strategic location. Answer the following questions about the Suez Canal. Use a print or online map of Africa and other resources, if needed.

1. What two bodies of water does the Suez Canal connect?

   _____

2. What two cities are at the ends of the Suez Canal?

   _____

3. List the countries that have had control of the Suez Canal.

   _____

4. Before the canal was built, how did ships get from Europe to the Far East?

   _____

Africa 17

Africa can be divided into many different regions according to physical geography, culture, climate, industry, and so on. Match each geographical region to its description. Use a print or online map of Africa or other resources, if needed.

_____ 1. North Africa	**A.**	Peninsula in East Africa that juts into the Arabian Sea
_____ 2. Horn of Africa	**B.**	Rain forest area in a large depression drained by the Congo River
_____ 3. Sahel	**C.**	Countries bordering the Mediterranean Sea and the northern edge of the Sahara
_____ 4. Congo Basin	**D.**	Transitional area of grasslands south of the Sahara
_____ 5. African Great Lakes	**E.**	Series of lakes in and around the East African Rift

Africa

Africa 18

European countries developed areas of influence as they colonized Africa. Identify the main European language spoken in each language region of Africa.

1. Francophone _____
2. Arabophone _____
3. Lusophone _____
4. Anglophone _____
5. Hispanophone _____

Africa 19

Unscramble the names of these native languages spoken in Africa. Use a print or online resource, showing the language regions of Africa.

1. GIRNE-CGONO _____
2. FOAR-SIITACA _____
3. NSKIHOA _____
4. ONSTAISRUENA

   _____
5. LHSWAII _____
6. TBANU _____
7. LION-NHRASAA _____
8. AMLOSI _____

Africa 20

In the word search below, find and circle 12 minerals found in Africa's mining regions.

```
D B F N V C T C A T
D E A O I U P O O I
I P D U H C D A R T
A I L U X T K L G A
M Z R A C I V E O N
O L I O T O T W L I
N E R N N I P E D U
D A Q U C O N P Q M
S D D H N S R U E Q
U R A N I U M E M R
```

Africa 21

Using a map of Africa and what you have learned about the continent, think about the following questions. Answer on your own paper.

1. What cities or countries would you like to visit for a beach vacation?

2. What cities or countries would you like to visit for a rain forest adventure?

3. What cities or countries would you like to visit to learn about history?

Africa

Africa 22

Use the clues and a map of Africa to decide which country is which.

1. I border the Indian Ocean.
    I am north of Mozambique.
    My capital starts with a "D."
    I am _____.

2. I am in western Africa.
    I am south of Mali and north of Ghana.
    My capital has 3 "O's" in it.
    I am _____.

Africa 23

Use the clues and a map of Africa to decide which country is which.

1. I am one of the smallest nations in Africa. I am between 20° and 30° south latitude. My name has nine letters.
    I am _____.

2. I border the Gulf of Guinea and the Atlantic Ocean.
    I am west of the Ivory Coast.
    My capital starts with an "M."
    I am _____.

Africa 24

Use a print or online map of Africa to match these countries with their capitals.

A. Rabat	B. Addis Ababa	C. Nairobi	D. Tripoli
E. Accra	F. Bamako	G. Abuja	H. Khartoum
I. Mogadishu	J. Asmara	K. Cairo	L. Nouakchott
M. Antananarivo	N. Luanda		

____ 1. Sudan   ____ 2. Libya   ____ 3. Madagascar

____ 4. Morocco   ____ 5. Mali   ____ 6. Egypt

____ 7. Ethiopia   ____ 8. Somalia   ____ 9. Ghana

____ 10. Angola   ____ 11. Kenya   ____ 12. Eritrea

____ 13. Mauritania   ____ 14. Nigeria

Antarctica

Antarctica 1

Fill in the blanks.

Antarctica is the world's southernmost (1) _____.
It surrounds the (2) _____ _____, which is the earth's most southern point. Antarctica means "opposite the (3) _____." The (4) _____ Mountains divide the continent into West Antarctica and East Antarctica. It is almost completely covered by a huge sheet of (5) _____.

Antarctica 2

Match the physical features with the numbers on the map.

___ Ronne Ice Shelf   ___ Ross Ice Shelf
___ Antarctic Peninsula   ___ South Pole
___ Eastern Antarctica
___ Western Antarctica

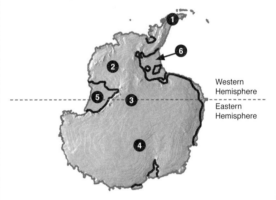

Western
Hemisphere

Eastern
Hemisphere

Antarctica 3

Match the bodies of water with the numbers on the map.

___ Weddell Sea   ___ Southern Ocean
___ Atlantic Ocean   ___ Pacific Ocean
___ Amundsen Sea   ___ Ross Sea
___ Bellingshausen Sea

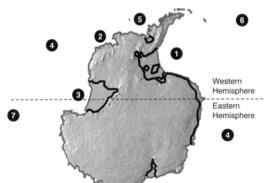

Western
Hemisphere

Eastern
Hemisphere

Antarctica 4

Unscramble the words in the description of Antarctica's relative location.

Antarctica is 600 miles (1,000 km) from (1) **u h t s o   e m i a a c r**

_____ _____.

It is 2,500 miles (4,000 km) from (2) **i c f a r a** _____, and 1,600 miles (2,500 km) from (3) **s a i a t l u a r** _____.

Antarctica

Antarctica 5

Use a print or online map of Antactica to answer the following questions.

1. What mountains cross through the middle of Antarctica?

   _____

2. What is the name of the peninsula in Antarctica that juts out near the southern tip of South America?

   _____

Antarctica 6

Use a print or online map of Antactica to answer the following question.

What are the names of four ice shelves in Antarctica?

_____

_____

_____

_____

Antarctica 7

Match each place to the weather described.

A. Commonwealth Bay
B. Vostok Station
C. Antarctic Peninsula

____ **1.** Windiest place in the world
____ **2.** Warmest place in Antarctica
____ **3.** Place with the coldest recorded temperature in the world

Antarctica 8

1. During what season does the interior of Antarctica have almost constant daylight?

   _____

2. During what season does the interior of Antarctica have almost constant darkness?

   _____

Antarctica

Antarctica 9

Match each type of ice to its description.

_____ 1. pack ice   **A.** moving masses of ice on land

_____ 2. ice sheet   **B.** large floating piece of permanent ice

_____ 3. glaciers   **C.** freezing seawater makes this

_____ 4. ice shelf   **D.** free-floating masses of ice

_____ 5. icebergs   **E.** thick layer of ice on top of a landmass

Antarctica 10

Unscramble the following words about glaciers in Antarctica.

1. As new snow falls, it presses **d l e o r** _____ snow into the ice sheet.
2. Glaciers move from the **t i r i n e r o** _____ of the continent toward the coast.
3. Glaciers move by the force of **a t v y i r g** _____.
4. The largest glacier is the **m b a l r t e** _____ Glacier.
5. The fastest-moving glacier is the **e r h i s a s** _____ Glacier.

Antarctica 11

Match each mountain peak to its description. Use an online or print map of Antarctica, if needed.

_____ 1. Mount Erebus   **A.** tallest mountain in Antarctica

_____ 2. Mount Kirkpatrick   **B.** southern-most active volcano in the world

_____ 3. Vinson Massif   **C.** highest dormant volcano in Antarctica

_____ 4. Mount Jackson   **D.** called Dinosaur Mountain for the fossils found there

_____ 5. Mount Sidley   **E.** highest mountain in the Antarctic Peninsula

Antarctica

Antarctica 12

There are no permanent human residents of Antarctica. During the summer, there are about 3,700 people doing scientific research. About 1,200 remain through the winter. On your own paper, write at least one thing each type of scientist could study in Antarctica.

1. paleontologist
2. climatologist
3. glaciologist
4. psychologist
5. physicist

Antarctica 13

Using online or print resources, write what country operates each permanent research station in Antarctica.

1. Jang Bogo _____
2. Rothera _____
3. Vostok _____
4. Troll _____
5. Amundsen-Scott South Pole

   _____
6. Zhongshan _____
7. Arctowski _____
8. Concordia _____
9. Davis _____
10. Maitri _____

Antarctica 14

With about 4,000 researchers and over 40,000 tourists in some years, a lot of waste can be generated on Antarctica. Efforts are being made to do a better job of cleaning up and preserving the environment for the native wildlife. Name some waste items you think might be left behind on Antarctica.

_____

_____

_____

_____

_____

Antarctica 15

Environmentalists are concerned that in the future, nations may try to mine or drill for mineral resources. Unscramble the resources that have been found in Antarctica.

1. NIRO ROE _____
2. RPCPEO _____
3. DOLG _____
4. RILVSE _____
5. CIENLK _____
6. ANIUPTLM _____
7. LOAC _____
8. BCOLAT _____

Antarctica

Antarctica 16

Many explorers tried to be the first to reach the South Pole. Match each explorer to their description.

____ **1.** Robert Falcon Scott
____ **2.** Roald Amundsen
____ **3.** Ernest Shackleton
____ **4.** Richard Byrd
____ **5.** John Davis

A. First person to set foot on Antarctica

B. Led first attempt to reach South Pole; died on his second attempt

C. First person to reach South Pole

D. Led failed expedition in 1908–09

E. First person to fly over South Pole

Antarctica 17

On December 1, 1959, 12 nations signed the Antarctic Treaty, which made the continent a non-military zone for scientific research. List some reasons why a country might have wanted to establish a military base in Antarctica.

_____

_____

_____

_____

_____

Antarctica 18

Four species of penguins breed and live on Antarctica or the surrounding islands for at least part of the year. They feed on krill and fish in the waters around Antarctica.

Unscramble the names of the four penguin species.

1. DIAELE _____

2. SATHRNPCI _____

3. TGEOON _____

4. PEOERMR _____

Antarctica 19

Many animals migrate to Antarctica in the summer months to feed on other animals. Fill in the food chain blanks below for marine life in the waters of Antarctica. Start at the bottom and work your way to the top of the food chain.

penguin	**phytoplankton**
killer whale	**krill** **seal**

5. _____

4. _____

3. _____

2. _____

1. _____

Antarctica

Antarctica 20

Seven countries have made territorial claims in Antarctica, but they abide by the Antarctic Treaty. Uscramble the names of the seven countries.

1. AIENRATNG _____
2. UALARSAIT _____
3. TNIUDE GNKDIMO
   _____
4. LEHIC _____
5. CFERAN _____
6. NWE DAEZLNA
   _____
7. ANWROY _____

Antarctica 21

Researchers have recently identified 15 distinct biogeographic regions in Antarctica. They examined data in the following areas. On your own paper, define what each term means.

1. geography
2. geology
3. climate
4. biology
5. flora
6. fauna
7. biodiversity

Antarctica 22

The 15 distinct Antarctic Conservation Biogeographic Regions of the ice-free areas of Antarctica are listed below. Go online and find a map of Antarctica showing the regions. Place the number for each region in the correct location on the map below.

1. North-east Antarctic Peninsula
2. South Orkney Islands
3. North-west Antarctic Peninsula
4. Central South Antarctic Peninsula
5. Enderby Land
6. Dronning Maud Land
7. East Antarctica
8. North Victoria Land
9. South Victoria Land
10. Transantarctic Mountains
11. Ellsworth Mountains
12. Marie Byrd Land
13. Adélie Land
14. Ellsworth Land
15. South Antarctic Peninsula

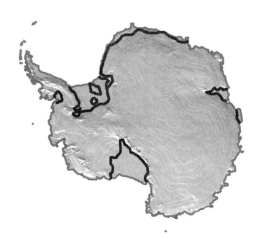

Antarctica

Antarctica 23

Write *T* for true or *F* for false.

____ **1.** 98% of Antarctica is covered with thick ice.

____ **2.** There are no lakes or rivers in Antarctica.

____ **3.** The highest peak in Antarctica is Vinson Massif.

____ **4.** The South Pole is the coldest, windiest, and driest place on Earth.

____ **5.** The Prime Meridian meets the International Date Line in Antarctica.

Antarctica 24

Write *T* for true or *F* for false.

____ **1.** Antarctica is smaller than the United States.

____ **2.** Antarctica has no native human residents.

____ **3.** Penguins live in Antarctica.

____ **4.** Polar bears live in Antarctica.

____ **5.** Antarctica is considered a desert.

Antarctica 25

Find and circle the following plants and animals in the word search puzzle. All of these can be found in Antarctica or its waters at least part of the year.

ALBATROSS   ALGAE   FUNGI   GULL

HAIRGRASS   KRILL   LICHEN   MOSS

PEARLWORT   PENGUIN   PETREL

SEAL   SKUA   TERN   WHALE

```
S L A E S C S L G P O T
K L L P U Q S V E U R Q
U I I E E A A T L O L E
A R C X L N R I W F L L
C K H H D E G L G A Q T
L R E Z L G R U H N E L
P T N T Q A I W I R U D
K L D F E L A S N N M F
A Q I P D T H E A G L A
A L B A T R O S S W U O
K H S P E Q V M O S S V
V Z C K J P T D B A H Q
```

Asia

Asia 1

For each set of latitude and longitude coordinates given, tell in what country in Asia it is located. Use a print or online atlas to help you.

1. 20° N, 80° E _____
2. 60° N, 110° E _____
3. 20° N, 50° E _____
4. 40° N, 90° E _____
5. 40° N, 140° E _____
6. 50° N, 70° E _____
7. 40° N, 40° E _____
8. 10° N, 120° E _____

Asia 2

Use a map of Asia from a print or online atlas to help you answer the questions.

1. What bay lies off the east coast of India? _____
2. What mountain in Asia is the highest mountain in the world? _____
3. Circle all of these that cross through Asia.
   **Equator   Tropic of Cancer
   Tropic of Capricorn**
4. What landform is the country of Japan? _____

Asia 3

Use a map of Asia from a print or online atlas to help you find the answers.

1. Name the three oceans that surround Asia. _____
   _____
   _____

2. Name five seas that are part of Asia. _____
   _____
   _____
   _____
   _____

Asia 4

Use a map of Asia from a print or online atlas to help you find the answers.

1. Name a country that separates China and Russia.

   _____

2. Name a country in Asia that has a part that is also in Europe.

   _____

Asia

Asia 5

Use a map of Asia from a print or online atlas to help you find the answers.

1. What country is directly south of Afghanistan? _____

2. What country is directly north of Yemen? _____

3. What country is directly west of Iran? _____

4. What country is directly east of Cambodia? _____

Asia 6

Tell in which country each of these Asian rivers is located. If it is in more than one country, list all the countries through which the river flows. Use a print or online atlas to help you locate the rivers.

1. Yangtze _____
2. Huang _____
3. Indus _____
4. Ganges _____
5. Tigris _____
6. Euphrates _____
7. Mekong _____
   _____

Asia 7

Match the countries with their capitals. Use a map of Asia from a print or online atlas to help you.

A. Ashgabat **B. Tokyo** **C. Manila**   **D. Astana** **E. Kabul**
F. Bangkok **G. Beijing** **H. Taipei**   **I. Tbilisi** **J. Muscat**
K. Ulan Bator **L. Kathmandu**   **M. New Delhi** **N. Baghdad**

____ 1. China   ____ 2. India

____ 3. Philippines   ____ 4. Oman

____ 5. Turkmenistan   ____ 6. Iraq

____ 7. Afghanistan   ____ 8. Japan

____ 9. Mongolia   ____ 10. Thailand

____ 11. Georgia   ____ 12. Kazakhstan

____ 13. Nepal   ____ 14. Taiwan

Asia

Asia 8

Match each place in Asia with its description.

_____ **1.** Caspian Sea

_____ **2.** Lake Baikal

_____ **3.** Plateau of Tibet

_____ **4.** Mount Everest

_____ **5.** Yangtze

A. world's highest point

B. Asia's longest river

C. world's deepest lake

D. referred to as "the roof of the world"

E. world's largest lake

Asia 9

Uscramble these mountain ranges and plateaus in Asia.

1. HALMAYIA _____

2. AURL _____

3. AILTA _____

4. SRZAOG _____

5. EDNCAC _____

6. ELCRATN   ISEBNIAR

_____

7. EBNITAT _____

8. PAUETLA   FO   INRA

_____

Asia 10

Circle the letter of the correct answer.

1. What animal is unique to China?

    A. freshwater seals
    B. giant pandas
    C. Komodo dragons
    D. Bactrian camels

2. What animal is unique to Borneo and Sumatra?

    A. Bactrian camels
    B. reindeer
    C. giant pandas
    D. orangutans

Asia 11

Circle the letter of the correct answer.

1. Which is NOT a major product harvested in the forests of Asia?

    A. bananas
    B. bamboo
    C. teak
    D. mahogany

2. Bauxite, a mineral found in India and Indonesia, is used in the production of

    A. steel.
    B. iron ore.
    C. aluminum.
    D. furniture.

Asia

Asia 12

Next to each country listed below, write *I* if it is an island or group of islands, *P* if it is on a peninsula, or *L* if it is a landlocked country.

____ **1.** Sri Lanka   ____ **2.** Uzbekistan   ____ **3.** Japan

____ **4.** Vietnam   ____ **5.** Nepal   ____ **6.** South Korea

____ **7.** Philippines   ____ **8.** Mongolia   ____ **9.** Thailand

____ **10.** Indonesia   ____ **11.** India   ____ **12.** Laos

____ **13.** Tajikistan   ____ **14.** Taiwan   ____ **15.** North Korea

Asia 13

Use the clues to determine which country or place in Asia is described.

1. I am the largest desert in Asia. I am located in northern China and Mongolia. My name starts with a "G." I am _____.

2. I am a country north of Iraq and Syria. I border the Mediterranean Sea. My capital is Ankara. I am _____.

3. I am a sea near Kazakhstan and Turkmenistan. I separate Europe and Asia. My name starts with a "C." I am _____.

4. I am an island just south of India. I am in the Indian Ocean. My capital is Colombo. I am _____.

Asia 14

Match the description to the animal or term found in Asia.

____ **1.** Komodo dragon   **A.** member of the crocodile family

____ **2.** snow leopards   **B.** disease transmitted by mosquitoes

____ **3.** Lake Baikal   **C.** make their homes in the highlands of

____ **4.** gavial   Central Asia

____ **5.** malaria   **D.** world's largest lizard

E. home of freshwater seals

Asia

Asia 15

Match each item concerning Asia's industries with the correct description.

_____ **1.** rubber _____ **2.** fish

_____ **3.** rice _____ **4.** Siberia

_____ **5.** Japan

A. world's leading fishing country

B. source of protein in most Asian diets

C. major crop of southeast Asia

D. product of large estate farms

E. steel production center

Asia 16

Laos is a **land-locked** country. This means that all of its borders are land. It has no direct contact with any ocean or  sea. Describe how products might be inported and exported without having access to a coast.

_____

_____

_____

_____

Asia 17

Many Asian nations, especially in the Middle East, have desert climates. Place a check mark next to the items below that are an adaptation to living in the desert.

_____ **1.** Using camels for transportation

_____ **2.** Wearing dark clothing

_____ **3.** Building houses with thick walls

_____ **4.** Living close to rivers

_____ **5.** Growing rice and sugar cane

_____ **6.** Drilling wells for irrigation

Asia 18

Circle the letter of the correct answer.

1. What mountains divide Russia into Asian and European parts?

    A. Himalayas
    B. Appalachians
    C. Urals
    D. Andes

2. This part of Russia is known as being cold, with poor soil and little population.

    A. Caucasus
    B. Siberia
    C. Russian Plain
    D. Black Sea Coast

Asia

Asia 19

Fill in the blanks with words from the word bank to make the information correct.

percent   season   winds   rainfall

The word *monsoon* means "season of the _____."
Generally the summer monsoon _____ in India takes place from June to September. It is a season of heavy _____ that brings as much as ninety _____ of the year's precipitation.

Asia 20

Match each item concerning Asia's culture with the correct description.

____ 1. Taj Mahal
____ 2. *Ramayana*
____ 3. Peking Opera
____ 4. pentatonic
____ 5. Bunraku

A. a musical scale of five notes
B. Japan's famous puppet theater
C. Indian building with an Islamic influence
D. Chinese performing arts group
E. great epic poem of India

Asia 21

Write the country from which each of these ideas or items have spread to the rest of the world.

1. acupuncture _____
2. Christianity _____
3. Bollywood films _____
4. Islam _____
5. Periodic Table _____
6. anime _____
7. Santa Claus _____
8. postal system _____
9. batik fabric dying _____

Asia 22

Write *M* if the item encouraged the movement of people, ideas, and products across Asia and the world, or write *B* if the item blocked movement.

____ 1. Great Wall of China
____ 2. the spice trade
____ 3. the Silk Road
____ 4. Japanese seclusion laws
____ 5. Himalaya Mountains
____ 6. radio and television
____ 7. Trans-Siberian Railway
____ 8. living on an island
____ 9. Yangtze River (Chang)
____ 10. Internet connection

Asia

Asia 23

Match the Asian climate terms with the correct descriptions.

____	1.	continental climate	**A.** winters are dry, summers often have monsoons
____	2.	monsoon	
____	3.	humid subtropical climate	**B.** cold winters and warm summers
____	4.	tundra	**C.** permanently frozen subsoil
____	5.	Mediterranean climate	**D.** mild climate year round
			E. a wind

Asia 24

Match the Middle-Eastern countries with the correct descriptions.

____	1.	Turkey	**A.** largest nation on the Arabian Peninsula
____	2.	Jordan	**B.** site of the Tigris and Euphrates River valleys
____	3.	Saudi Arabia	**C.** about 75% of its population is Jewish
____	4.	Syria	**D.** important link to Europe and Asia
____	5.	Israel	**E.** fighting a civil war and ISIS terrorists
____	6.	Iraq	**F.** became independent from Britain in 1946

Asia 25

Circle the correct answers for these questions about the Far East.

1. What country is now divided into two nations?
   A. Korea   **B.** China   **C.** Taiwan   **D.** Vietnam

2. It is a major center for trade and banking.
   A. Japan   **B.** Hong Kong   **C.** Mongolia   **D.** Taiwan

3. What is the name of the early Japanese military leaders?
   A. Ninjas   **B.** Princes   **C.** Moguls   **D.** Shoguns

Australia & Oceania

Australia & Oceania 1

Use maps of Australia and Oceania from a print or online atlas to help you identify by letter the following locations.

_____ **1.** Indian Ocean

_____ **2.** Southern Ocean

_____ **3.** Great Barrier Reef

_____ **4.** Tasman Sea

_____ **5.** Arafura Sea

_____ **6.** Bass Strait

_____ **7.** Gibson Desert

_____ **8.** Great Dividing Range

_____ **9.** Cook Strait

_____ **10.** Solomon Islands

Australia & Oceania 2

Use maps of Australia and Oceania from a print or online atlas to help you answer the questions.

1. What line passes through Oceania and determines what day it is?

_____

2. Which island is divided between two countries—one in Asia and one in Oceania?_____

3. Which island country is actually two islands, a north island and a south island?_____

Australia & Oceania 3

Next to each city or place tell on which island or island group in Oceania it is located. Use print or online maps of Australia and Oceania to help you.

1. Canberra _____

2. Port Moresby _____

3. Honiara _____

4. Port Vila _____

5. Suva _____

6. Nuku'alofa _____

7. Hobart _____

8. Majuro _____

9. Sydney _____

10. Auckland _____

Australia & Oceania

Australia & Oceania 4

Using a map of Australia from a print or online atlas, label the states and territories on the map of Australia at right.

New South Wales   **Queensland**

South Australia   **Victoria**

Western Australia   **Tasmania**

Australian Capital Territory

Northern Territory

Australia & Oceania 5

Find each set of coordinates on maps of Australia and Oceania from a print or online atlas and then determine which island in each list is closest to that place.

1. 40° S, 170° E
    (a.) Samoa   (b.) New Zealand   (c.) Papua New Guinea
2. 20° S, 180°
    (a.) Fiji   (b.) Tasmania   (c.) Marshall Islands
3. 20° S, 140° E
    (a.) Australia   (b.) New Zealand   (c.) Tuvalu
4. 0°, 160° E
    (a.) Tonga   (b.) Australia   (c.) Nauru

Australia & Oceania 6

Use the map of **New Zealand** to help you answer the questions.

1. Is the capital city of Wellington on the north or south island? _____

2. What waterway separates the north and south islands? _____

3. To go from Greymouth to Dunedin, which direction would you travel? _____

4. What smaller island is just south of the south island? _____

Australia & Oceania

Australia & Oceania 7

Match the Australian place with its description.

_____ 1. outback
_____ 2. Tasmania
_____ 3. Mount Kosciuszko
_____ 4. Australia
_____ 5. Murray

A. island off the south coast of Australia
B. world's smallest continent
C. interior region of the continent
D. major river that flows through the Central Lowlands
E. Australia's highest mountain

Australia & Oceania 8

Use a print or online atlas to unscramble these bodies of water around Australia.

1. URRAAAF EAS
   _____
2. LROCA ASE
   _____
3. EGRTA TASAALNIRU GHBIT
   _____
4. ULFG FO CTEPAIANRAR
   _____
5. NADINI COEAN
   _____
6. APCIFCI NCEOA
   _____
7. AMSANT ESA
   _____
8. IMRTO SAE
   _____

Australia & Oceania 9

Circle the letter of the correct answer.

1. What are Australia's national colors?

   A. green and white
   B. black and gold
   C. green and gold
   D. red and white

2. Which one is not an official language of New Zealand?

   A. English
   B. Portugese
   C. Maori
   D. New Zealand Sign Language

Australia & Oceania 10

Match each term with its description.

_____ 1. Union Jack
_____ 2. prime minister
_____ 3. "Advance Australia Fair"
_____ 4. Canberra
_____ 5. Australia Day

A. the British flag
B. head of the Australian government
C. capital city of Australia
D. national holiday of Australia
E. national anthem of Australia

Australia & Oceania

Australia & Oceania 11

Match the items related to the economy of Australia and Oceania at the top to the correct examples at the bottom.

A. Agriculture   **B.** Mining

C. Manufacturing

___ **1.** barley   ___ **2.** bauxite

___ **3.** beef   ___ **4.** paper

___ **5.** machinery ___ **6.** textiles

___ **7.** tungsten ___ **8.** wheat

___ **9.** wool   ___ **10.** zinc

Australia & Oceania 12

Circle the animals below that were non-native species, brought to Australia.

cassowary   rabbit

bandicoot   emu

kangaroo   horse

wombat   pig

fox   echidna

penguin   crocodile

cane toad   camel

dingo   water buffalo

Australia & Oceania 13

Match the item associated with the Aboriginal people of Australia with the correct definition.

___ **1.** totem

___ **2.** nomadic tribes

___ **3.** dingoes

___ **4.** clan

___ **5.** boomerang

A. returns to its starting point when thrown correctly

B. did not build permanent villages

C. family group

D. object used as an emblem

E. animal used for hunting

Australia & Oceania 14

Fill in the blanks with words from the box.

| east   outback   coast |
| irrigation   mined |

Most of Australia's population lives near the _____. This is because the interior is a dry, rocky place called the _____. As winds blow from the east to west, they drop precipitation on the _____ side of the mountains. Minerals are _____ in the interior. Farmers use _____ to water crops in much of Australia's farmland.

Australia & Oceania

Australia & Oceania 15

Unscramble the words in the paragraph.

The first people to live in Australia are called (1) **l i g a o r b i n a** _____ Australians. They may have migrated from (2) **i s a a** _____ over 40,000 years ago. The (3) **o i a r m** _____ migrated to New Zealand from (4) **n p o s a i e y l** _____ over 700 years ago. Many of the first European settlers were British (5) **c t i s v n c o** _____ sent to Australia as punishment.

Australia & Oceania 16

Order the sequence of events in Australia from (1) first to (6) last.

____ 1. First European settlement
____ 2. The Dutch explored.
____ 3. Aboriginal peoples arrived.
____ 4. The Commonwealth of Australia was formed.
____ 5. James Cook landed.
____ 6. Gold was discovered.

Australia & Oceania 17

People from Asia and Polynesia have settled on many of the islands in the Pacific Ocean. Find the names of these islands in the word search below.

Nauru   Samoa   Palau   Tonga Kiribati   Tuvalu   Vanuatu   Fiji Micronesia

```
U T A U N A V Q E E H Z J M N S R
D R P A L A U Q D T F X O X A A V
N P R Y B Q T L E T X N H E U M A
X F P C O O X I M S O I G Z R O O
J W R P U K Y H X E V N J H U A P
R W W K I R I B A T I O G I M P G
Q L A I S E N O R C I M O A F L I
I G W B Y Z C Q T W T U V A L U J
```

Australia & Oceania 18

Australia's rivers provide transportion for people and products, water for irrigation, hydroelectric power, and recreational opportunities. On your own paper, write in which Australian states or territories each river flows.

1. Flinders River
2. Darling River
3. Murray River
4. Victoria River
5. Murrumbidgee River
6. South Esk River
7. Gascoyne River
8. Cooper Creek
9. Goulburn River
10. Diamantina River

Australia & Oceania

Australia & Oceania 19

Place the letter of the word that would make the statement correct on the blank in the statement.

1. The islands of the _____ can be divided into three areas.
2. *Melanesia* means "_____ islands."
3. *Micronesia* means "_____ islands."
4. *Polynesia* means "_____ islands."
5. Some islands have fewer than _____ people.
6. There are islands in the Pacific with _____ people.

A. tiny
B. 100
C. zero
D. Pacific
E. many
F. black

Australia & Oceania 20

Use a print or online map of Oceania to help you identify if the island or island group is in Melanesia (*ML*), Micronesia (*MC*) or Polynesia (*P*).

___ 1. Pitcairn Islands   ___ 2. Vanuatu   ___ 3. Cook Islands

___ 4. Marshall Islands   ___ 5. Guam   ___ 6. Samoa

___ 7. Solomon Islands   ___ 8. Fiji   ___ 9. Palau

___ 10. Northern Mariana Islands   ___ 11. Tonga

___ 12. New Caledonia   ___ 13. Papua New Guinea

___ 14. Kiribati   ___ 15. American Samoa

Australia & Oceania 21

Answer the questions about Australia's major geographic regions.

1. Along which coast does the Great Dividing Range run? _____
2. What island state off the south coast is considered a separate region?

    _____
3. The Central Lowlands includes what area where a huge amount of water is stored underground? _____
4. The great deserts of Australia are in what geographic region?

    _____

Australia & Oceania

Australia & Oceania 22

Match the term relating to Australia's climate regions to the correct description.

_____ 1. Tasmania

_____ 2. savanna

_____ 3. temperate climate

_____ 4. desert

_____ 5. tropical climate

A. has four distinct seasons

B. has hot, wet season and hot, dry season

C. grasses of this climate region support large herds of sheep and cattle

D. about two-thirds of the continent that receives less than ten inches of rain a year

E. has a marine west coast climate

Australia & Oceania 23

Match the term relating to Australia's plants to the correct description.

_____ 1. acacia

_____ 2. golden wattle

_____ 3. wheat

_____ 4. pine forests

_____ 5. eucalyptus

A. Australia's major export crop

B. grow along the east coast and in Tasmania

C. Australia's national flower

D. used for curing toothaches and healing wounds

E. used in antiseptics and cough medicine

Australia & Oceania 24

Most of Australia's population lives in urban areas near the coast. Almost two-thirds of its people live in eight cities, each with a population of over 100,000. However, there are many small cities and towns in the interior region of Australia. Use a print or online map of Australia to help you identify if the city is a large urban area (*U*) or a small coastal or outback town (*S*).

_____ 1. Adelaide   _____ 2. Coober Pedy   _____ 3. Melbourne

_____ 4. Broken Hill   _____ 5. Beechworth   _____ 6. Perth

_____ 7. Alice Springs   _____ 8. Brisbane   _____ 9. Sydney

_____ 10. Canberra   _____ 11. Broome   _____ 12. Cygnet

Europe

Europe 1

Using a print or online map of Europe, find each set of latitude and longitude coordinates given. Tell in what country or place in Europe it is located.

1. 60° N, 50° E _____
2. 60° N, 10° E _____
3. 50° N, 30° E _____
4. 50° N, 20° E _____
5. 50° N, 10° E _____
6. 40° N, 0° _____
7. 50° N, 10° W _____
8. 40° N, 6° E _____

Europe 2

Use world and Europe maps from a print or online atlas to help you answer the questions.

1. What major mountain range separates the European and Asian parts of Russia? _____
2. What mountain range separates Norway and Sweden?

_____

3. What mountain range runs along the borders of Italy, France, and Switzerland? _____

Europe 3

Use world and Europe maps from a print or online atlas to help you answer the questions.

1. What two oceans surround Europe? _____
2. Name three countries in Europe that are islands. _____
_____
3. What bay lies between France and Spain? _____
4. What major river runs through Russia? _____

Europe 4

Use a map of Europe from a print or online atlas to help you answer the questions.

1. What country in Europe is shaped like a boot and sticks out into the Mediterranean Sea?
_____
2. What three countries border Spain? _____
_____
5. What country lies west of Romania and east of Austria?
_____

Europe

Europe 5

Match these countries in Europe with their capitals. Use a map of Europe from a print or online atlas if you need help.

___	**1.** Portugal	___	**9.** Ukraine	**A. Copenhagen**	**I. Madrid**
___	**2.** Spain	___	**10.** Greece	**B. Reykjavik**	**J. Budapest**
___	**3.** Iceland	___	**11.** Finland	**C. Athens**	**K. Dublin**
___	**4.** Ireland	___	**12.** Sweden	**D. Kiev**	**L. Berlin**
___	**5.** Russia	___	**13.** Norway	**E. Oslo**	**M. Helsinki**
___	**6.** Germany	___	**14.** Hungary	**F. Rome**	**N. Lisbon**
___	**7.** Italy	___	**15.** Belarus	**G. Stockholm**	**O. Moscow**
___	**8.** Poland	___	**16.** Denmark	**H. Minsk**	**P. Warsaw**

Europe 6

Use a map of Europe to help you unscramble the words that complete each statement.

1. **e r e c g e** _____ lies west of Turkey across the Aegean Sea.
2. Latvia, Estonia, and Sweden all border the **l t a b c i** _____ Sea.
3. **u i s r a s** _____ is the largest country in Europe.
4. The **h z c e c** _____ Republic is bordered on the north by Poland and Germany.

Europe 7

Match the geographical feature with the correct description.

___   **1.** Iberian Peninsula
___   **2.** Russia
___   **3.** Mount Blanc
___   **4.** Volga
___   **5.** Lake Ladoga

A. country located in Europe and Asia
B. Europe's largest freshwater lake
C. Europe's longest river
D. location of Spain and Portugal
E. one of Europe's most famous mountains

Europe

Europe 8

Use the map of France to answer the following questions.
Fill in the bubble of the correct answer.

1. Which body of water is located west of France?
   (a.) Bay of Biscay   (b.) Mediterranean Sea
2. The capital city of Paris is located in what part of France?
   (a.) Southwestern   (b.) Southeastern   (c.) Northern
3. Which city is located near the coast of the Mediterranean Sea?
   (a.) Montpelier   (b.) Bordeaux   (c.) Dijon
4. Which of these countries borders France on the east?
   (a.) Spain   (b.) United Kingdom   (c.) Switzerland

Europe 9

Find the names of these major rivers in Europe in the word search.

Danube   **Don**
Elbe   **Loire**
Po   **Oder**
Rhine   **Rhone**
Shannon **Thames**
Volga

G	G	R	I	S	W	I	F	V	O	L	G	A	H	C	S	O
R	N	N	G	P	E	P	V	M	O	L	F	X	E	M	S	G
H	R	H	K	H	I	R	Y	D	N	D	K	K	N	O	E	P
X	R	E	R	H	I	N	E	S	H	A	N	N	O	N	M	V
V	V	U	D	O	N	R	W	U	X	N	U	Y	H	O	A	D
R	Q	V	P	O	H	M	S	I	F	U	F	M	R	R	H	K
E	R	I	O	L	Y	N	O	B	V	B	S	V	V	L	T	G
Q	P	E	L	B	E	J	N	F	V	E	J	D	B	Y	Q	K

Europe 10

Write the name of the correct city next to each description.
     Rome   Venice   Florence

1. Borders the **Adriatic Sea** _____

2. Is the largest city in Italy _____

3. Has a canal system _____

4. Home of many **Renaissance artists** _____

5. Was the center of the **Roman Empire** _____

6. Is in north central Italy _____

Europe

Europe 11

Use the clues and a map of Europe to help you determine the place.

1. I am a country that borders the Adriatic Sea. I lie southwest of Hungary. My capital is Zagreb. I am _____.

2. I am a country between the Ukraine and Romania. My capital is Chisinau. I am a landlocked country. I am _____.

Europe 12

Use the clues and a map of Europe to help you determine the place.

1. I am an island country northwest of the United Kingdom. I am just south of the Arctic Circle. My capital is Reykjavik. I am _____.

2. I'm an island in the Mediterranean Sea. I am off the west coast of Italy and the southern coast of France. I belong to France and start with a "C." I am _____.

Europe 13

Match each term related to Europe's animals to the correct description.

____ 1. Loch Ness
____ 2. chamois
____ 3. Low Countries
____ 4. Lapland
____ 5. British Isles

A. noted for their fine woolen products
B. reindeer are common here
C. small goat-like antelope
D. lake in Scotland where a legendary monster may live
E. Belgium, the Netherlands, and Luxembourg

Europe 14

Circle the letter of the correct answer. Use online or print resources to help you, if needed.

1. What are the main agricultural products in western Europe?
   A. wheat and olives
   B. dairy and meat
   C. corn and beans
   D. potatoes and rye

2. Which European countries are noted as sources of cork?
   A. Spain and Portugal
   B. Germany and France
   C. Sweden and Norway
   D. Finland and Poland

Europe

Europe 15

Match the term related to Europe's economy to the correct description.

____ 1. Euro
____ 2. Industrial Revolution
____ 3. European Union
____ 4. North Sea
____ 5. agriculture

A. major fields of oil and natural gas are found here
B. organization created to improve trade
C. the major currency of Europe
D. a major industry of Europe
E. Europe first became a leader in manufacturing during this era

Europe 16

Many European capitals were established on the banks of rivers. As the cities have grown, they have expanded to both sides of the river. Match these capital cities to the rivers that flow through them.

____ 1. Budapest   A. Spree
____ 2. Paris   B. Thames
____ 3. Moscow   C. Amstel
____ 4. Dublin   D. Seine
____ 5. Rome   E. Tiber
____ 6. Amsterdam   F. Moskva
____ 7. Berlin   G. Danube
____ 8. London   H. Liffey

Europe 17

Answer the following questions about Europe's culture and innovation.

1. Who created the first major road system in Europe? _____
2. Where was ballet developed? _____
3. What dance was made famous in Vienna, Austria? _____
4. Who is Europe's most famous playwright? _____
5. Where was opera introduced? _____
6. The Colosseum is an example of ancient architecture in what city? _____

Europe 18

Match the term related to Europe's language to the correct description.

____ 1. Indo-European
____ 2. Balto-Slavic
____ 3. Germanic-based
____ 4. Romantic-based

A. languages spoken in eastern Europe
B. languages spoken in northern Europe
C. most European languages belong to this family
D. languages spoken in southern Europe

Europe

Europe 19

Opportunities for the movement of goods, people, and ideas within and through Europe have been the greatest in the world. Unscramble the following terms related to movement in Europe.

1. AERDT _____
2. RESPEOLRX _____
3. RVESRI _____
4. ANMTIGIRO _____
5. CNSAEO _____
6. SELUNAAGG _____
7. SRWA _____
8. GILSORNIE _____
9. ARASLIDOR _____
10. NZLIICOOOATN _____
11. EICTADNUO _____
12. CEOHYNGLOT _____

Europe 20

Fill in the bubble of the correct answer.

1. What two countries are connected by the Chunnel?
   a. France and Spain b. England and France c. Italy and France
2. What city was divided by a wall after World War II and reunited in 1990?
   a. Budapest b. Prague c. Berlin
3. What former country's provinces have become independent nations?
   a. Poland b. Yugoslavia c. Bulgaria
4. Vikings sailing from this country were the first to settle in Greenland.
   a. Iceland b. Sweden c. Finland

Europe 21

Many European countries set up colonies in developing regions of the world in the past. They governed these regions, traded with them, and influenced their language and culture. Answer the questions about European colonization.

1. What language do the people of Brazil speak? _____
2. Libya was a colony of what European nation for many years? _____
3. Canada was claimed by which two European nations?

   _____

4. What country controlled the Chinese city-state of Hong Kong for over 150 years? _____

Europe

Europe 22

Regions are drawn according to things such as geography, race, language, religion, politics, and history. Some of Europe's regions include Scandinavia, the Baltic States, and the Balkans. Put each of these countries in the region where it belongs.

Denmark	Romania	Lithuania	Greece	Sweden	Croatia
Albania	Latvia	Norway	Bulgaria	Estonia	Iceland

Scandinavia	Balkans	Baltic States
1. _____	1. _____	1. _____
2. _____	2. _____	2. _____
3. _____	3. _____	3. _____
4. _____	4. _____	
	5. _____	

Europe 23

Climate regions stretch across many different countries, which means they have similar weather patterns. Write the correct climate region next to the description.

1. Influenced by the sea and the Alps, which block colder air, much of Spain, southern France, Italy, and Greece share this climate.

   _____

2. Moderate climate north of the Alps that receives warm, moist breezes from the Atlantic Ocean

   _____

Europe 24

The British Isles are an island region that is considered part of Europe. Match the following countries and descriptions.

____ 1. Scotland
____ 2. England
____ 3. Northern Ireland
____ 4. Wales
____ 5. The Republic of Ireland

A. separate from the United Kingdom
B. the part of Ireland in the UK
C. occupies the largest part of the island of Britain
D. borders on the west of England
E. noted for its highlands

North America

North America 1

Use a map of North America from a print or online atlas to answer these questions.

1. Name the oceans that border North America. _____

   _____

2. Name the gulf off the southeast coast of the United States.

   _____

3. Name the large bay in the northeastern part of Canada.

   _____

North America 2

Use a map of North America from a print or online atlas to answer these questions.

1. Name four North American countries located south of Mexico.

   _____

   _____

2. Is more of North America north or south of the Tropic of Cancer?

   _____

3. What country is east of Baffin Bay? _____

North America 3

Place each letter in the approximate area where each feature is found in North America. You may use more than one copy of the letter to indicate a feature that is found in more than one location. Use an atlas to help you.

A. **Rocky Mountains**   B. **Great Plains**

C. **Appalachian Mountains**

D. **Gulf of California**

E. **Mississippi River**   F. **Canadian Shield**

G. **Aleutian Islands**   H. **Caribbean Sea**

I. **Great Lakes**   J. **Gulf of Mexico**

North America

North America 4

Match each country with its capital. Use a print or online atlas if you need help.

A. **Belmopan**   B. **Panamá City**   C. **San José**   D. **San Salvador**
E. **Washington, D.C.**   F. **Ottawa**   G. **Nassau**   H. **Port-au-Prince**
I. **Guatemala City**   J. **Mexico City**   K. **Kingston**
L. **Tegucigalpa**   M. **Managua**

___ 1. United States   ___ 2. Canada   ___ 3. Mexico
___ 4. Belize   ___ 5. Guatemala   ___ 6. El Salvador
___ 7. Costa Rica   ___ 8. Nicaragua   ___ 9. Honduras
___ 10. Haiti   ___ 11. Panama   ___ 12. Jamaica
___ 13. Bahamas

North America 5

By each island name, write a *GA* if it is one of the **Greater Antilles** or *LA* if it is one of the **Lesser Antilles**. Use an atlas if you need help locating the islands.

___ 1. **Cuba**   ___ 2. **Barbuda**
___ 3. **Aruba**   ___ 4. **Grenada**
___ 5. **Haiti**   ___ 6. **Barbados**
___ 7. **U.S. Virgin Islands**
___ 8. **Jamaica**   ___ 9. **St. Vincent**
___ 10. **Montserrat**   ___ 11. **Martinique**
___ 12. **Puerto Rico** ___ 13. **Dominican Republic**

Greater Antilles

Lesser Antilles

North America 6

What am I?

1. I am the longest river in the United States. I flow from north to south. I empty into the Gulf of Mexico. _____

2. I am a large lake in Manitoba, Canada. I am not one of the Great Lakes. I am southwest of Hudson Bay. _____

3. I am a canal that allows passage from the Pacific Ocean to the Caribbean Sea. I am almost on the southern tip of North America. _____

North America

North America 7

Canada has ten provinces and three territories. Unscramble their names and write the answers on your own paper. Use a print or online map of Canada, if needed.

1. RAAETLB   2. AORTOIN
3. WEN BUWCIKNRS
4. RTBIHIS MALOIBUC
5. UATUVNN
6. WNRTOEHTS OTRTRIRESEI
7. SAHASEKANWCT
8. IERNPC ARDWED IALNDS
9. OEFNWLNDUAND
10. BQCEUE   11. NMOAIBAT
12. UYKNO ORTRYRETI
13. AVON TCAOSI

North America 8

Match the terms related to Canada with the correct descriptions.

____ 1. Inuit
____ 2. Quebec
____ 3. Vancouver
____ 4. French
____ 5. Rocky Mountains

A. official language of Quebec
B. major port on the Pacific Ocean
C. cover most of British Columbia's land
D. native people of Canada
E. Canada's largest province

North America 9

Fill in the blanks to make the statements about the United States true.

1. The longest river in the U.S. is the _____.
2. The highest point in the U.S. is _____.
3. The lowest point in the U.S. is _____.
4. The state with part of its land above the arctic circle is _____.
5. The state that consists of islands in the Pacific is _____.

North America 10

Match the terms related to Mexico with the correct descriptions.

____ 1. Mexico
____ 2. Aztecs
____ 3. *Estados Unidos Mexicanos*
____ 4. Mexico City
____ 5. Acapulco

A. Mexico's capital
B. official name of Mexico in Spanish
C. resort city
D. largest Spanish-speaking country in the world
E. ancient civilization of Mexico

North America

North America 11

Circle the letter of the correct answer.

1. Which Central American country has the most stable government?

    A. Belize   **B.** Honduras
    C. Costa Rica   **D.** Nicaragua

2. What is Belize's official language?

    A. Spanish   **B.** English
    C. French   **D.** German

3. Which is Central America's most densely populated nation?

    A. El Salvador **B.** Belize
    C. Guatemala   **D.** Panama

North America 12

Unscramble the island that fits each clue.

1. Covered with sheet glaciers
   ELDNGERNA

   _____

2. Largest island in the West Indies
   BACU _____

3. Group of islands in the Atlantic
   ABAMSHA

   _____

4. Two nations share this island
   NPILAHSOI

   _____

North America 13

Match the environment that is best for each type of occupation.

____ 1. The Great Plains
____ 2. The Rocky Mountains
____ 3. California's Central Valley
____ 4. The Gulf of Mexico
____ 5. The waters off Greenland

A. Drilling for oil
B. Mining
C. Fishing
D. Grain farming
E. Growing fruit trees

North America 14

Fill in the blanks with words from the box to make each statement true.

mills	**flood**	**transportation**
hydroelectric		

1. The rivers of North America provide a means of

   _____ for

   people and goods.

2. Early dams provided _____ control and power for _____ that ground grain.

3. Many of today's dams produce

   _____ power.

North America

North America 15

Use the bar graph to answer the following questions.

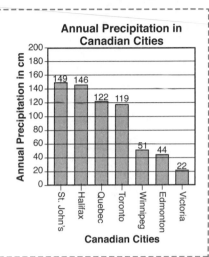

Annual Precipitation in Canadian Cities

1. In which cities would sales of umbrellas and raincoats be high? _____
_____

2. In which cities might unnecessary water use be restricted during parts of the year?
_____

North America 16

As people turned from agriculture to other industries, they moved to cities. Fit these North American cities into the correct spots in the crossword puzzle.

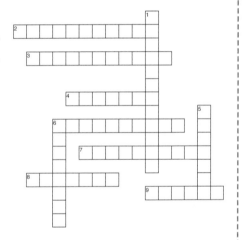

New York City   **Mexico City**

Los Angeles   **Chicago**

Toronto   **Houston**

Guadalajara   **Montreal**

Santo Domingo   **Havana**

North America 17

Use the map and information to help you answer the questions.

Costa Rica Dimensions	
North to South: 354 km	East to West: 382 km
Caribbean coastline: 214 km	Pacific coastline: 612 km

1. Which is a better estimate for the distance from Tortuguero to Pandora?

   368 km   112 km   198 km

2. Which is a better estimate for the distance from Coco to Tortuguero?

   380 km   350 km   278 km

North America

North America 18

Since the first people came to North America, they have felt the need to travel from one part of the continent to another. List some of the ways people have traveled the continent throughout history.

_____

_____

_____

_____

_____

_____

North America 19

Answer these questions about the Panama Canal.

1. What two bodies of water are connected by the Panama Canal?

_____

2. The direction of travel is mostly _____ and _____.

3. What land formation does the canal cross? _____

4. Where did ships going from the Atlantic to the Pacific have to sail before the canal was built?

_____

North America 20

Match each Great Lake with the correct description.

____ 1. Lake Superior
____ 2. Lake Huron
____ 3. Lake Michigan
____ 4. Lake Erie
____ 5. Lake Ontario

A. only lake completely within the U.S.
B. flows into the St. Lawrence River
C. site of American victory in a War of 1812 naval battle
D. contains "Shipwreck Coast" where many ships have sunk
E. contains the world's largest freshwater island and beach

North America 21

Unscramble these climate regions of North America.

1. AOIPLRCT _____
2. MUDHI IOATTCLNNNE

_____

3. RCBCTIUAS _____
4. TARNMANREEEDI

_____

5. ARDNUT _____
6. EEDSTR _____
7. IEMRAN TEWS CATSO

_____

8. IHALGNDH _____

North America

North America 22

Match the climate region to the correct description.

___ **1.** semi-desert
___ **2.** highland
___ **3.** tropical
___ **4.** humid continental
___ **5.** Mediterranean

A. has hot temperatures and much rainfall throughout the year

B. has hot daytime temperatures with cool nights and very little rainfall

C. has mild winters and warm summers

D. has moderate temperatures and adequate rainfall

E. includes cold winters and hot summers, with adequate amounts of precipitation

North America 23

Write the letter of the region on the map next to the correct name below.

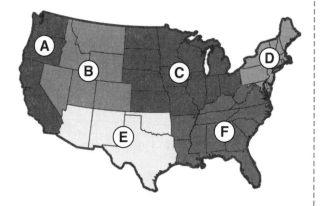

___ **1.** Northeast
___ **2.** Southeast
___ **3.** Midwest
___ **4.** Mountain
___ **5.** Southwest
___ **6.** Pacific

North America 24

Find and circle these physical regions of North America in the puzzle.

Canadian Shield   **Coastal Plain**
Interior Lowlands   **Great Plains**
Rocky Mountains   **Antilles Arc**
Coastal Ranges   **Great Lakes**
Mexican Highlands
Central American Ranges
Intermountain Plateaus
Appalachian Mountains

```
R R A A E C U L A S L N U C U O G T L L S
S N I A T N U O M N A I H C A L A P P A A
I S E I O I D E H M D S G O O K S I A R I
L E X I O A N N L I A T G A O A U R T G I
N R O N A S G R G L H L H O L I L R A N K
A N S C T A I E I N E R N K A S L R T A H
S U A E T A L P N I A T N U O M R E T N I
S E G N A R N A C I R E M A L A R T N E C
N P Y A R O C K Y M O U N T A I N S N L O
I R I A S A G T R P E N U L O A A E S R A
A N A S K A N S L A M N N R N A H G G C S
L M E X I C A N H I G H L A N D S N R A T
P I C E P T T U S G O O N I A A N A E U A
T A S K I W M P A S W N S A T T S R A L L
A O N C A O L N N L A E R M I E N L T I P
E I C A N A D I A N S H I E L D T A L L L
R R A C R N I N G L L S C L E A E T A K A
G A N A L M D H N I T L I O M W I S K I I
C P E R A S D N I A S T D L D C C A E I N
U S A T I L A E S A N G G E A L L O S P E
A K D A T S U I R A E S N U D L S C A X E
```

South America

South America 1

Use a print or online atlas to help you answer the questions.

1. Name three South American countries through which the equator passes.

   _____

   _____

2. Name three South American countries that border the Caribbean Sea.

   _____

   _____

South America 2

Use a print or online atlas to help you answer the questions.

1. What country in South America has the largest coastline?

   _____

2. Name the two landlocked countries in South America

   _____

   _____

3. Name the only South American country that lies completely south of the Tropic of Capricorn.

   _____

South America 3

Circle the letter of the correct answer.

1. What line nearly cuts South America in half?

   A. equator
   B. Tropic of Capricorn
   C. Tropic of Cancer

2. What connects South America to Central and North America?

   A. Isthmus of Panama
   B. Tropic of Cancer
   C. Amazon River

3. Lima, Peru, is _____ of Miami, Florida.

   A. west   B. north   C. east

South America 4

Find the name of the major city nearest the latitude and longitude given. Then tell in what country it is located. Use a print or online atlas to help you.

Location	City, Country
1. 22° S, 43° W	_____
2. 31° S, 64° W	_____
3. 13° S, 71° W	_____
4. 16° S, 68° W	_____
5. 10° N, 72° W	_____
6. 6° N, 75° W	_____
7. 53° S, 70° W	_____
8. 34° S, 56° W	_____

South America

South America 5

Use an atlas to help you match the capitals with their countries.

____ 1. Argentina	**A. Asunción**
____ 2. Bolivia	**B. Bogotá**
____ 3. Brazil	**C. Caracas**
____ 4. Chile	**D. Georgetown**
____ 5. Colombia	**E. Santiago**
____ 6. Ecuador	**F. La Paz**
____ 7. French Guiana	**G. Lima**
____ 8. Guyana	**H. Cayenne**
____ 9. Paraguay	**I. Paramaribo**
____ 10. Peru	**J. Buenos Aires**
____ 11. Suriname	**K. Brasilia**
____ 12. Uruguay	**L. Montevideo**
____ 13. Venezuela	**M. Quito**

South America 6

Use an atlas to help you answer the questions.

1. What major river runs west to east through northern South America? _____

2. What mountain range runs north to south along the western edge of South America?

   _____

3. What lake straddles the border between Peru and Bolivia?

   _____

South America 7

Use an atlas to help you answer the questions.

1. What basin lies primarily in northern Brazil?

   _____

2. What islands lie off the east coast of southern Argentina?

   _____

3. What islands lie off the west coast of Ecuador? _____

   _____

South America

South America 8

Use a map of Peru to help complete the activity.

1. What river is in northwest Peru?
   _____
2. What lake is on the border with Bolivia? _____
3. What major mountain range runs north to south in the middle of Peru? _____
4. What city is near the mouth of the Amazon River? _____

South America 9

Write *T* for true or *F* for false.

____ 1. Brazil is the second largest country in South America.

____ 2. The capital of Brazil is Rio de Janeiro.

____ 3. Manaus is a city on the Amazon River.

____ 4. A large portion of Brazil has a tropical climate.

____ 5. The primary language spoken in Brazil is Spanish.

____ 6. Brazil borders every country in South America except Ecuador and Chile.

South America 10

Unscramble these South American rivers.

1. NPAARA _____
2. AGURPYAA _____
3. AMRAEDI _____
4. ZAMNOA _____
5. OCNOIRO _____
6. EMGLANDAA

   _____
7. NXUIG _____
8. ASO ICOCASRNF

   _____

South America 11

Match the place with its description.

____ 1. Angel Falls

____ 2. Amazon

____ 3. Titicaca

____ 4. Andes

____ 5. Aconcagua

A. world's longest mountain range

B. Western Hemisphere's highest point

C. world's highest waterfall

D. South America's longest river

E. world's highest navigable lake

South America

South America 12

Fill in the blanks with words from the word bank to make the information correct.

Amazon	average	canopy	forests
afternoon	nighttime	rain	temperatures

More than one-third of South America is covered by rain _____.
The majority of the _____ River Basin is dense forest. The daytime
_____ are usually in the 90s, and _____
temperatures are in the 70s. As the temperatures rise in the _____,
thunderstorms develop and heavy _____ falls almost every day. In one
year, an _____ of 103 inches falls in the rain forest.
The rain forest has several layers. Tall trees form a _____
over the ground below.

South America 13

Fill in the blanks with words from the word bank to make the information correct.

Chile	roads	capital	knots
civilizations	structures	Quito	medicine

There were numerous early _____ all over South America.
One of the most famous were the Incas. The Inca Empire lasted from A.D. 1400
to 1532. It stretched from present-day _____, Ecuador, down the west
coast of South America to the middle of _____. The Inca _____
was the city of Cuzco, Peru. The Incas built a large network of stone _____
and had expert builders who cut stones by hand and built _____
without mortar. Though they had no written language, they developed a counting
system using quipus with _____ tied on strings. They made advances
in _____ and created beautiful art.

South America

South America 14

Beside each fact about Chile put a *P* if it is a physical characteristic or an *H* if it is a human characteristic.

___ **1.** The primary language in Chile is Spanish.
___ **2.** The Andes Mountains separate Chile from Argentina.
___ **3.** From north to south, Chile is about 4,260 kilometers long.
___ **4.** The main religion in Chile is Roman Catholic.
___ **5.** The bottom tip of Chile is one of the world's wettest and stormiest places.
___ **6.** The favorite sport in Chile is soccer.
___ **7.** Chile is rich in minerals such as copper, silver, and gold.

South America 15

Match the term related to South America's industries to the correct description.

___ **1.** Venezuela
___ **2.** petroleum
___ **3.** Incas
___ **4.** forests
___ **5.** processing agricultural products

A. South America's major industry
B. first mined gold in the Andes Mountains
C. cover over half of South America
D. has most of South America's petroleum reserves
E. one of the major sources of energy

South America 16

There are many unique species of plants and animals found in South America and on its islands. Efforts are being made to preserve the habitats of these species. Do an online search for each species and circle the plant or animal if it is an endangered species from South America.

huacaya alpaca	blond capuchin monkey	big leaf mahogany
monkey brush vine	blunt-eared bat	toco toucan
West Indian manatee	green anaconda	hanging lobster claw flower
giant otter	brown-throated sloth	giant prickly pear cactus
ocelot	Andean wax palm	silver vase bromeliad

South America

South America 17

South America was colonized by European nations, and the languages of these countries spread to the colonies. Match the European language to the country where it is an official language today.

A. English   **B.** Spanish   **C.** Dutch
D. Portuguese   **E.** French

__ **1.** Venezuela   __ **2.** Brazil
__ **3.** Suriname   __ **4.** Guyana
__ **5.** French Guiana __ **6.** Chile
__ **7.** Argentina   __ **8.** Peru

South America 18

1. What ancient civilization flourished in the Andes Mountains and had a road system of over 12,000 milies?

   _____

2. What were the Spanish soldiers called who came to explore and conquer South America?

   _____

3. Where are the descendants of Portuguese settlers mostly found today?

   _____

South America 19

The music and dance of South America have formed from a blend of native, European, and African influences. Many of these forms have become popular throughout the world. Draw a line matching each dance to the country where it originated.

1. caporales	Peru
2. marinera	Brazil
3. tango	Ecuador
4. cumbia	Paraguay
5. joropo	Argentina
6. samba	Bolivia
7. danza de la botella	Venezuela
8. pasillo	Colombia

South America 20

Most of the population of South America lives near the coast. From large port cities on the Pacific, Atlantic, and Caribbean coasts, goods and people travel all over the world. Unscramble these port cities.

1. ENOMVDETIO _____

2. ICPCEOOCNN _____

3. ECERIF _____

4. GEGNTORWOE _____

5. IOR ED IOJERAN _____

6. NUOESB REISA _____

7. LPIVSAROAA _____

8. IALM _____

South America

South America 21

1. What is the climate of central Chile with warm, dry summers and mild, wet winters?

   _____

2. What type of climate is most of the Amazon River Basin?

   _____

3. What type of climate is the southern part of Chile?

   _____

4. What climate type is in northwest Argentina, near the mountains?

   _____

South America 22

Match each vegetation or physical region in Argentina to its description.

____ 1. Patagonia
____ 2. Pampas
____ 3. Chaco
____ 4. Mesopotamia
____ 5. Cuyo

A. fertile grassland in the central-east
B. mountainous wine country of the central-west
C. hot, semi-arid forested region of the north
D. area of lush vegetation between the Paraná and Uruguay Rivers
E. area of sparse vegetation in the south

South America 23

Circle the letter of the correct answer.

1. Where do most people live in Chile?

   A. Patagonia
   B. Atacama Desert
   C. Central Valley

2. What is the high flat area in the Andes where most Bolivians live?

   A. Altiplano Plateau
   B. Pampas
   C. Central Valley

3. The Paraguay River divides Paraguay into what two regions?

   A. Northern/Southern
   B. Eastern/Western

South America 24

Write an F on the blank if the statement is a fact or an O if it is an opinion.

____ 1. The Andes Mountains were home to the Incas.

____ 2. Life in the Andes Mountains is lonely and difficult.

____ 3. The Galápagos Islands have the most beautiful national parks in the world.

____ 4. Ecuador controls the Galápagos Islands.

____ 5. The Amazon rain forest is the world's largest tropical rain forest.

____ 6. More land in the rain forest should be protected.

Answer Keys

Geography Terms & Map Skills 1 (p. 2)

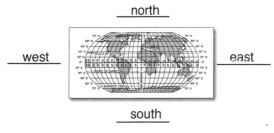

north

west

east

south

Geography Terms & Map Skills 2 (p. 2)
1. longitude   2. latitude

Geography Terms & Map Skills 3 (p. 2)
1. C   2. B   3. A

Geography Terms & Map Skills 4 (p. 2)
1. E   2. D   3. A   4. C   5. B   6. G
7. F

Geography Terms & Map Skills 5 (p. 3)
1. political   2. land
3. physical   4. road

Geography Terms & Map Skills 6 (p. 3)
1. 500   2. 75   3. 31.5

Geography Terms & Map Skills 7 (p. 3)

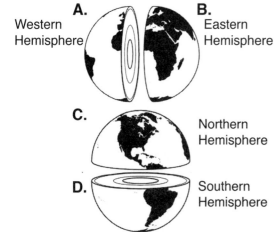

A.
Western
Hemisphere

B.
Eastern
Hemisphere

C.
Northern
Hemisphere

D.
Southern
Hemisphere

Geography Terms & Map Skills 8 (p. 3)
1. SCALE   2. LATITUDE
3. COMPASS   4. LEGEND
5. POLITICAL   6. PHYSICAL
7. LONGITUDE   8. DEGREES
9. BORDERS   10. OCEANS

Geography Terms & Map Skills 9 (p. 4)

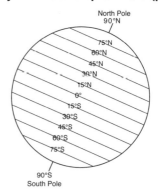

Geography Terms & Map Skills 10 (p. 4)

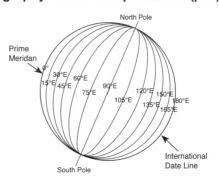

Geography Terms & Map Skills 11 (p. 4)
1. Chicago, IL
2. Cape Town, South Africa
3. Helsinki, Finland   4. Santiago, Chile

Geography Terms & Map Skills 12 (p. 4)
1. N   2. SW   3. E   4. S
5. NE   6. W   7. NE   8. NW

Africa 1 (p. 5)
1. Madagascar   2. Morocco   3. South Africa

Africa 2 (p. 5)
1. *Lake Victoria:* straddles the borders of Uganda, Tanzania, and Kenya
2. *Drakensberg Mountains:* along the southeast side of South Africa, also in Lesotho
3. *Kalahari Desert:* in southern Botswana, northern South Africa, and eastern Namibia
4. *Gulf of Guinea:* area of the Atlantic Ocean near the equator and South of Ghana, Togo, Benin and Nigeria; west of Cameroon and Equatorial Guinea

5. *Nile River:* flows south to north through Uganda, South Sudan, Sudan, and Egypt into the Mediterranean Sea

Africa 3 (p. 5)
1. 37°N, 3°E   2. 16°N, 33°E   3. 34°N, 8°W
4. 15°S, 28°E   5. 8°N, 13°W   6. 34°S, 19°E
7. 1°S, 33°E   8. 3°S, 37°E

Africa 4 (p. 5)
1. Botswana   2. Tanzania
3. Zambia, Zimbabwe   4. Egypt
5. Ethiopia
6. Malawi, Mozambique, Tanzania

Africa 5 (p. 6)
1. D   2. R   3. R   4. D   5. R   6. R
7. D   8. D

Africa 6 (p. 6)
Algeria, Chad, Egypt, Libya, Mali, Mauritania, Morocco, Niger, Western Sahara, Sudan, Tunisia (also parts of Senegal, Eritrea, Nigeria, Burkina Faso)

Africa 7 (p. 6)
1. ZEBRA   2. LION
3. CHEETAH   4. ELEPHANT
5. GIRAFFE   6. WARTHOG
7. GAZELLE   8. OSTRICH

Africa 8 (p. 6)
1. TANGANYIKA   2. ABAYA
3. CHAMO   4. TURKANA
5. NATRON   6. ALBERT
7. MALAWI   8. EDWARD

Africa 9 (p. 7)
1. D   2. E   3. A   4. B   5. C

Africa 10 (p. 7)
1. *hunters:* They hunt animals for food and trade and use animal products for tools and shelter; live in forests or on the grassy plains.
2. *fishers:* They catch fish and other aquatic animals for food and trade; live near coasts, rivers, or lakes.
3. *planters:* They plant and grow crops for food and trade; live on the plains and near rivers where the soil is fertile and there is water.

Africa 11 (p. 7)
1. C   2. R   3. R   4. R   5. C
6. C   7. C   8. C   9. R   10. R

Africa 12 (p. 8)
1. C   2. E   3. A   4. B   5. D

Africa 13 (p. 8)
1. B   2. D   3. E   4. A   5. C

Africa 14 (p. 8)
Answers will vary by year and source used.

Africa 15 (p. 8)
1. France   2. Great Britain 3. Italy
4. Spain   5. Belgium   6. Germany
7. Portugal

Africa 16 (p. 9)
1. Mediterranean Sea and Red Sea
2. Port Said and Suez
3. France, Great Britain, Egypt
4. They sailed around the Cape of Good Hope.

Africa 17 (p. 9)
1. C   2. A   3. D   4. B   5. E

Africa 18 (p. 10)
1. French   2. Arabic   3. Portuguese
4. English   5. Spanish

Africa 19 (p. 10)
1. NIGER-CONGO   2. AFRO-ASIATIC
3. KHOSIAN   4. AUSTRONESIAN
5. SWAHILI   6. BANTU
7. NILO-SAHARAN   8. SOMALI

Africa 20 (p. 10)

Africa 21 (p. 10)
Answers will vary.

Africa 22 (p. 11)
1. Tanzania   2. Burkina Faso

Africa 23 (p. 11)
1. Swaziland   2. Liberia

Africa 24 (p. 11)
1. H   2. D   3. M   4. A   5. F   6. K
7. B   8. I   9. E   10. N   11. C   12. J
13. L   14. G

Antarctica 1 (p. 12)
1. continent   2. South Pole   3. arctic
4. Transantarctic   5. ice

Antarctica 2 (p. 12)
6 Ronne Ice Shelf   5 Ross Ice Shelf
1 Antarctic Peninsula   3 South Pole
4 Eastern Antarctica   2 Western Antarctica

Antarctica 3 (p. 12)
1 Weddell Sea   4 Southern Ocean
6 Atlantic Ocean   7 Pacific Ocean
2 Amundsen Sea   3 Ross Sea
5 Bellingshausen Sea

Antarctica 4 (p. 12)
1. South America   2. Africa   3. Australia

Antarctica 5 (p. 13)
1. Transantarctic Mountains
2. Antarctic Peninsula

Antarctica 6 (p. 13)
(Any four) Ross, Ronne-Filchner (or Ronne and Filchner), Shackleton, Amery, Larsen, Riiser-Larsen, Fimbul, George VI, West, Wilkins

Antarctica 7 (p. 13)
1. A   2. C   3. B

Antarctica 8 (p. 13)
1. summer (Southern Hemisphere)
2. winter (Southern Hemisphere)

Antarctica 9 (p. 14)
1. C   2. E   3. A   4. B   5. D

Antarctica 10 (p. 14)
1. older   2. interior   3. gravity
4. Lambert   5. Shirase

Antarctica 11 (p. 14)
1. B   2. D   3. A   4. E   5. C

Antarctica 12 (p. 15)
Answers will vary, but could include:
1. *paleontologist:* fossils
2. *climatologist:* study ice to see changes in climate; ozone hole
3. *glaciologist:* movement of the ice

4. *psychologist:* how humans react to the polar environment
5. *physicist:* the thin atmosphere allows for the study of auroras, cosmic rays, and radio waves

Antarctica 13 (p. 15)
1. South Korea   2. United Kingdom
3. Russia   4. Norway
5. United States   6. China
7. Poland   8. Italy and France
9. Australia   10. India

Antarctica 14 (p. 15)
Answers will vary.

Antarctica 15 (p. 15)
1. IRON ORE   2. COPPER   3. GOLD
4. SILVER   5. NICKEL   6. PLATINUM
7. COAL   8. COBALT

Antarctica 16 (p. 16)
1. B   2. C   3. D   4. E   5. A

Antarctica 17 (p. 16)
Answers will vary, but could include:
    It would make a good refueling stop. It could be used as a base for missile launches.

Antarctica 18 (p. 16)
1. ADELIE   2. CHINSTRAP
3. GENTOO   4. EMPEROR

Antarctica 19 (p. 16)
5. killer whale   4. seal   3. penguin
2. krill   1. phytoplankton

Antarctica 20 (p. 17)
1. ARGENTINA   2. AUSTRALIA
3. UNITED KINGDOM   4. CHILE
5. FRANCE   6. NEW ZEALAND
7. NORWAY

Antarctica 21 (p. 17)
Answers will vary, but could include:
1. *geography:* the study of the earth's physical features and its various climates, countries, peoples, and natural resources
2. *geology:* the study of the earth, the materials of which it is made, the structure of those materials, and the processes acting upon them
3. *climate:* the weather conditions prevailing in an area in general or over a long period

4. *biology:* the study of living organisms
5. *flora:* the plant life of a particular region, habitat, or geological period
6. *fauna:* the animals of a particular region, habitat, or geological period
7. *biodiversity:* the variety of life (number and types of species) in the world or in a particular habitat or ecosystem

Antarctica 22 (p. 17)

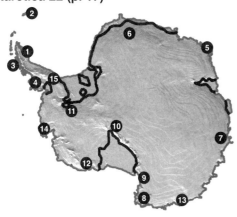

Antarctica 23 (p. 18)
1. T   2. F   3. T   4. T   5. T

Antarctica 24 (p. 18)
1. F   2. T   3. T   4. F   5. T

Antarctica 25 (p. 18)

Asia 1 (p. 19)
1. India   2. Russia   3. Saudi Arabia
4. China   5. Japan   6. Kazakhstan
7. Turkey   8. Philippines

Asia 2 (p. 19)
1. Bay of Bengal   2. Mt. Everest
3. Equator, Tropic of Cancer 4. islands

Asia 3 (p. 19)
1. Indian, Pacific, Arctic
2. Any seas in or surrounding Asia (e.g., Yellow Sea, East China Sea, Red Sea, etc.)

Asia 4 (p. 19)
1. Mongolia or Kazakhstan
2. Russia or Turkey

Asia 5 (p. 20)
1. Pakistan   2. Saudi Arabia
3. Iraq   4. Vietnam

Asia 6 (p. 20)
1. China   2. China
3. Pakistan   4. India, Bangladesh
5. Turkey, Iraq   6. Turkey, Syria, Iraq
7. Laos, China, Thailand, Cambodia, Myanmar, Vietnam

Asia 7 (p. 20)
1. G   2. M   3. C   4. J   5. A   6. N
7. E   8. B   9. K   10. F   11. I   12. D
13. L   14. H

Asia 8 (p. 21)
1. E   2. C   3. D   4. A   5. B

Asia 9 (p. 21)
1. HIMALAYA   2. URAL
3. ALTAI   4. ZAGROS
5. DECCAN   6. CENTRAL SIBERIAN
7. TIBETAN   8. PLATEAU OF IRAN

Asia 10 (p. 21)
1. B   2. D

Asia 11 (p. 21)
1. A   2. C

Asia 12 (p. 22)
1. I   2. L   3. I   4. P   5. L   6. P
7. I   8. L   9. P   10. I   11. P
12. L/P 13. L   14. I   15. P

Asia 13 (p. 22)
1. the Gobi Desert   2. Turkey
3. the Caspian Sea   4. Sri Lanka

Asia 14 (p. 22)
1. D   2. C   3. E   4. A   5. B

Asia 15 (p. 23)
1. D   2. B   3. C   4. E   5. A

Asia 16 (p. 23)
Answers will vary, but could include:
Products are shipped on rivers, trucks, or railways.

Asia 17 (p. 23)
Check #1, 3, 4, 6

Asia 18 (p. 23)
1. C   2. B

Asia 19 (p. 24)
winds, season, rainfall, percent

Asia 20 (p. 24)
1. C   2. E   3. D   4. A   5. B

Asia 21 (p. 24)
1. China   2. Israel   3. India
4. Saudi Arabia and the area that is now Israel
5. Russia   6. Japan
7. Turkey   8. Iran (Persia)
9. Indonesia

Asia 22 (p. 24)
1. B   2. M   3. M   4. B   5. B   6. M
7. M   8. B   9. M   10. M

Asia 23 (p. 25)
1. B   2. E   3. A   4. C   5. D

Asia 24 (p. 25)
1. D   2. F   3. A   4. E   5. C   6. B

Asia 25 (p. 25)
1. A   2. B   3. D

Australia & Oceania 1 (p. 26)
1. B   2. E   3. H   4. A   5. G   6. D
7. J   8. I   9. C   10. F

Australia & Oceania 2 (p. 26)
1. International Date Line
2. New Guinea   3. New Zealand

Australia & Oceania 3 (p. 26)
1. Australia   2. Papua New Guinea
3. Solomon Islands   4. Vanuatu/Efate
5. Fiji   6. Tonga/Tongatapu
7. Tasmania, Australia   8. Marshall Islands
9. Australia   10. New Zealand

Australia & Oceania 4 (p. 27)

Australia & Oceania 5 (p. 27)
1. b   2. a   3. a   4. c

Australia & Oceania 6 (p. 27)
1. North Island   2. Cook Strait
3. south   4. Stewart Island

Australia & Oceania 7 (p. 28)
1. C   2. A   3. E   4. B   5. D

Australia & Oceania 8 (p. 28)
1. ARAFURA SEA   2. CORAL SEA
3. GREAT AUSTRALIAN BIGHT
4. GULF OF CARPENTARIA
5. INDIAN OCEAN   6. PACIFIC OCEAN
7. TASMAN SEA   8. TIMOR SEA

Australia & Oceania 9 (p. 28)
1. C   2. B

Australia & Oceania 10 (p. 28)
1. A   2. B   3. E   4. C   5. D

Australia & Oceania 11 (p. 29)
1. A   2. B   3. A   4. C   5. C   6. C
7. B   8. A   9. A   10. B

Australia & Oceania 12 (p. 29)
rabbit, horse, pig, fox, cane toad, camel, water buffalo

Australia & Oceania 13 (p. 29)
1. D   2. B   3. E   4. C   5. A

Australia & Oceania 14 (p. 29)
coast, outback, east, mined, irrigation

Australia & Oceania 15 (p. 30)
1. Aboriginal   2. Asia   3. Maori
4. Polynesia   5. convicts

Australia & Oceania 16 (p. 30)
1. 4   2. 2   3. 1   4. 6   5. 3   6. 5

Australia & Oceania 17 (p. 30)

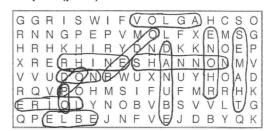

Australia & Oceania 18 (p. 30)
1. Queensland   2. New South Wales
3. New South Wales, Victoria, South Australia
4. Northern Territory
5. Australia Capital Territory, New South Wales
6. Tasmania   7. Western Australia
8. Queensland, South Australia   9. Victoria
10. Queensland, South Australia

Australia & Oceania 19 (p. 31)
1. D   2. F   3. A   4. E   5. B   6. C

Australia & Oceania 20 (p. 31)
Some answers may vary according to the map used.
1. P   2. ML   3. P   4. MC
5. MC   6. P   7. ML   8. ML
9. MC   10. MC   11. P   12. ML
13. ML   14. MC   15. P

Australia & Oceania 21 (p. 31)
1. east   2. Tasmania
3. Great Artesian Basin   4. Western Plateau

Australia & Oceania 22 (p. 32)
1. E   2. C   3. A   4. D   5. B

Australia & Oceania 23 (p. 32)
1. D   2. C   3. A   4. B   5. E

Australia & Oceania 24 (p. 32)
1. U   2. S   3. U   4. S   5. S   6. U
7. S   8. U   9. U   10. U   11. S   12. S

Europe 1 (p. 33)
1. Russia   2. Norway   3. Ukraine
4. Poland   5. Germany   6. Spain
7. Atlantic Ocean   8. Mediterranean Sea

Europe 2 (p. 33)
1. Urals 2. Kjølen (Scandinavian) 3. Alps

Europe 3 (p. 33)
1. Atlantic, Arctic
2. Ireland, Great Britain, Iceland
3. Bay of Biscay   4. Volga

Europe 4 (p. 33)
1. Italy   2. Portugal, France, Andorra
3. Hungary

Europe 5 (p. 34)
1. N   2. I   3. B   4. K   5. O   6. L
7. F   8. P   9. D   10. C   11. M   12. G
13. E   14. J   15. H   16. A

Europe 6 (p. 34)
1. Greece   2. Baltic   3. Russia   4. Czech

Europe 7 (p. 34)
1. D   2. A   3. E   4. C   5. B

Europe 8 (p. 35)
1. a   2. c   3. a   4. c

Europe 9 (p. 35)

Europe 10 (p. 35)
1. Venice   2. Rome   3. Venice
4. Florence   5. Rome   6. Florence

Europe 11 (p. 36)
1. Croatia   2. Moldova

Europe 12 (p. 36)
1. Iceland   3. Corsica

Europe 13 (p. 36)
1. D   2. C   3. E   4. B   5. A

Europe 14 (p. 36)
1. B   2. A

Europe 15 (p. 37)
1. C   2. E   3. B   4. A   5. D

Europe 16 (p. 37)
1. G   2. D   3. F   4. H   5. E   6. C
7. A   8. B

Europe 17 (p. 37)
1. the Romans   2. France   3. waltz
4. William Shakespeare   5. Italy   6. Rome

Europe 18 (p. 37)
1. C   2. A   3. B   4. D

Europe 19 (p. 38)
1. TRADE   2. EXPLORERS
3. RIVERS   4. MIGRATION
5. OCEANS   6. LANGUAGES
7. WARS   8. RELIGIONS
9. RAILROADS   10. COLONIZATION
11. EDUCATION   12. TECHNOLOGY

Europe 20 (p. 38)
1. b   2. c   3. b   4. a

Europe 21 (p. 38)
1. Portuguese   2. Italy
3. France and Great Britain
4. Great Britain (United Kingdom)

Europe 22 (p. 39)
In any order:
Scandinavia: Denmark, Sweden, Norway,
Iceland
Balkans: Romania, Greece, Croatia, Albania,
Bulgaria
Baltic States: Lithuania, Latvia, Estonia

Europe 23 (p. 39)
1. Mediterranean   2. marine west coast

Europe 24 (p. 39)
1. E   2. C   3. B   4. D   5. A

North America 1 (p. 40)
1. Atlantic, Pacific, Arctic
2. Gulf of Mexico   3. Hudson Bay

North America 2 (p. 40)
1. Any four: Guatemala, Belize, El Salvador,
   Honduras, Nicaragua, Costa Rica, Panama
2. north   3. Greenland

North America 3 (p. 40)

North America 4 (p. 41)
1. E   2. F   3. J   4. A   5. I   6. D
7. C   8. M   9. L   10. H   11. B   12. K
13. G

North America 5 (p. 41)
1. GA   2. LA   3. LA   4. LA   5. GA
6. LA   7. LA   8. GA   9. LA 10. LA
11. LA 12. GA 13. GA

North America 6 (p. 41)
1. Mississippi River   2. Lake Winnipeg
3. Panama Canal

North America 7 (p. 42)
1. ALBERTA   2. ONTARIO
3. NEW BRUNSWICK
4. BRITISH COLUMBIA   5. NUNAVUT
6. NORTHWEST TERRITORIES
7. SASKATCHEWAN
8. PRINCE EDWARD ISLAND
9. NEWFOUNDLAND   10. QUEBEC
11. MANITOBA   12. YUKON TERRITORY
13. NOVA SCOTIA

North America 8 (p. 42)
1. D   2. E   3. B   4. A   5. C

North America 9 (p. 42)
1. Mississippi River   2. Denali
3. Death Valley, CA   4. Alaska 5. Hawaii

North America 10 (p. 42)
1. D   2. E   3. B   4. A   5. C

North America 11 (p. 43)
1. C   2. B   3. A

North America 12 (p. 43)
1. GREENLAND   4. CUBA
2. BAHAMAS   5. HISPANIOLA

North America 13 (p. 43)
1. D   2. B   3. E   4. A   5. C

North America 14 (p. 43)
1. transportation   2. flood, mills
3. hydroelectric

North America 15 (p. 44)
1. St. John's, Halifax, Quebec, Toronto
2. Victoria, Edmonton, Winnipeg

North America 16 (p. 44)

North America 17 (p. 44)
1. 198 km   2. 380 km

North America 18 (p. 45)
Answers will vary, but could include: walking; riding horses; wagons pulled by horses, mules, or oxen; stagecoach; canoes; boats; sailing ships; steamships; locomotives; automobiles; airplanes

North America 19 (p. 45)
1. Caribbean Sea (Atlantic Ocean) and Pacific Ocean
2. north, south   3. Isthmus of Panama
4. around Cape Horn

North America 20 (p. 45)
1. D   2. E   3. A   4. C   5. B

North America 21 (p. 45)
1. TROPICAL   2. HUMID CONTINENTAL
3. SUBARCTIC   4. MEDITERRANEAN
5. TUNDRA   6. DESERT
7. MARINE WEST COAST 8. HIGHLAND

North America 22 (p. 46)
1. B   2. C   3. A   4. E   5. D

North America 23 (p. 46)
1. D   2. F   3. C   4. B   5. E   6. A

North America 24 (p. 46)

```
R R A A E C U L A S L N U C U O G T L L S
S N I A T N U O M N A I H C A L A P P A A
I S E I O I D E H M D S G O O K S I A R I
L E X I O A N N L I A T G A O A U R T G I
N R O N A S G R G L H L H O L I L R A N K
A N S C T A I E I N E R N K A S L R T A H
S U A E T A L P N I A T N U O M R E T N I
S E G N A R N A C I R E M A L A R T N E C
N P Y A R O C K Y M O U N T A I N S N L O
I R I A S A G T R P E N U L O A A E S R A
A N A S K A N S L A M N N R N A H G G O S
L M E X I C A N H I G H L A N D S N R A T
P I C E P T T U S G O O N I A A N A E U A
T A S K I W M P A S W N S A T T S R A L L
A O N C A O L N N L A E R M E N L T I P
E I C A N A D A N S H I E L D T A L L L L
R R A C R N N G L L S C L E A E T A K A
G A N A L M D H N I T L I O M W I S K I I
C P E R A S D N I A S T D L D C C A E I N
U S A T I L A E S A N G G E A L L O S P E
A K D A T S U I R A E S N U D L S C A X E
```

South America 1 (p. 47)
1. Ecuador, Colombia, Brazil
2. Venezuela, Colombia, Suriname, Guyana, French Guiana (any three)

South America 2 (p. 47)
1. Brazil   2. Bolivia, Paraguay
3. Uruguay

South America 3 (p. 47)
1. B   2. A   3. C

South America 4 (p. 47)
1. Rio de Janeiro, Brazil
2. Cordoba, Argentina
3. Cuzco, Peru
4. La Paz, Bolivia
5. Maracaibo, Venezuela
6. Medellin, Colombia
7. Punta Arenas, Chile
8. Montevideo, Uruguay

South America 5 (p. 48)
1. J   2. F   3. K   4. E   5. B   6. M
7. H   8. D   9. A   10. G   11. I   12. L
13. C

South America 6 (p. 48)
1. Amazon River   2. Andes
3. Lake Titicaca

South America 7 (p. 48)
1. Amazon Basin   2. Falkland Islands
3. Galápagos Islands

South America 8 (p. 49)
1. Marañón   2. Lake Titicaca
3. the Andes   4. Iquitos

South America 9 (p. 49)
1. F   2. F   3. T   4. T   5. F   6. T

South America 10 (p. 49)
1. PARANA   2. PARAGUAY
3. MADEIRA   4. AMAZON
5. ORINOCO   6. MAGDALENA
7. XINGU   8. SAO FRANCISCO

South America 11 (p. 49)
1. C   2. D   3. E   4. A   5. B

South America 12 (p. 50)
forests, Amazon, temperatures, nighttime,
afternoon, rain, average, canopy

South America 13 (p. 50)
civilizations, Quito, Chile, capital, roads,
structures, knots, medicine

South America 14 (p. 51)
1. H   2. P   3. P   4. H   5. P   6. H
7. P

South America 15 (p. 51)
1. D   2. E   3. B   4. C   5. A

South America 16 (p. 51)
blond capuchin monkey, big leaf mahogany,
blunt-eared bat, West Indian manatee,
giant otter, giant prickly pear cactus,
Andean wax palm

South America 17 (p. 52)
1. B   2. D   3. C   4. A   5. E   6. B
7. B   8. B

South America 18 (p. 52)
1. Incas   2. Conquistadors   3. Brazil

South America 19 (p. 52)
1. caporales: Bolivia
2. marinera: Peru
3. tango: Argentina
4. cumbia: Colombia
5. joropo: Venezuela
6. samba: Brazil
7. danza de la botella: Paraguay
8. pasillo: Ecuador

South America 20 (p. 52)
1. MONTEVIDEO   2. CONCEPCION
3. RECIFE   4. GEORGETOWN
5. RIO DE JANEIRO 6. BUENOS AIRES
7. VALPARAISO   8. LIMA

South America 21 (p. 53)
1. Mediterranean   2. tropical
3. marine west coast 4. steppe

South America 22 (p. 53)
1. E   2. A   3. C   4. D   5. B

South America 23 (p. 53)
1. C   2. A   3. B

South America 24 (p. 53)
1. F   2. O   3. O   4. F   5. F   6. O

Bibliography

Activities may have been previously published in the following Mark Twain Media, Inc. books:

Barden, Cindy and Wendi Silvano. (2017) *Geography Warm-Ups.*

Kramme, Michael with Schyrlet Cameron and Carolyn Craig, consultants. (2012) *Continents of the World Geography Series. (Africa, Antarctica, Asia, Australia, Europe, North America,* and *South America.)*

Shireman, Myrl. (2012) *Map Reading Skills.*

Stange, Mark A. and Rebecca Laratta. (2015) *World Geography: Explore Your World.*